Pretty Tripwire

Pretty Tripwire

ALESSANDRA LYNCH

Alice James Books
Farmington, Maine
www.alicejamesbooks.org

10 9 8 7 6 5 4 3 2 1

Alice James Books are published by Alice James Poetry Cooperative, Inc., an affiliate of the University of Maine at Farmington.

Alice James Books
114 Prescott Street
Farmington, ME 04938
www.alicejamesbooks.org

Library of Congress Cataloging-in-Publication Data

Names: Lynch, Alessandra, 1965- author.
Title: Pretty tripwire / Alessandra Lynch.
Description: Farmington, ME : Alice James Books, [2021]
Identifiers: LCCN 2020016860 (print) | LCCN 2020016861 (ebook) | ISBN
    9781948579148 (trade paperback) | ISBN 9781948579872 (epub)
Subjects: LCGFT: Poetry.
Classification: LCC PS3612.Y54 P74 2021 (print) | LCC PS3612.Y54 (ebook)
    | DDC 811/.6--dc23
LC record available at https://lccn.loc.gov/2020016860
LC ebook record available at https://lccn.loc.gov/2020016861

Alice James Books gratefully acknowledges support from individual donors, private foundations, the University of Maine at Farmington, the National Endowment for the Arts, the Amazon Literary Partnership, and the Maine Arts Commission, an independent state agency supported by the National Endowment for the Arts.

Cover artwork by Valerie Hegarty

Contents

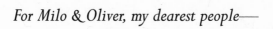

For Milo & Oliver, my dearest people—

In a dark time, the eye begins to see,
I meet my shadow in the shade;
I hear my echo in the echoing wood—

What falls away is always and is near

—Theodore Roethke

Supplication

This time, empty, unnourished, unnourishable, you will enter the arctic
room of the skull,

> its two large windows, asbestos walls, its sea

of icy shards cascading,

> this time enter
> though the fish carcass with its stunned mouth
> is riding the hard heavy waves

as if alive.

> Small indispensable mouth of fate.

This time enter with the slow care you learned
from stroking a dog's bony head, his immolated eyes
taking you in,

> this time
> with awareness that damage has been done to your mind, has been
done to you—

> and this sea is a shattering, unlike glass, more like Flower shattering,
so quiet the remnants, the ruin, you yourself couldn't hear, didn't know
exactly anything, the transaction, the event, a dreamy underfog.

This time kneel

in the currents, curling waves of cold petals, the familiar edges
serrated, stranger-ed, more cutting
than you remember.

    The pieces might never have been whole, taken shape, never been yours.
This time let the petals fatten on your tongue,
      ease down your throat—

      let them form a new organ,
something like the extra heart you needed
to love yourself someone said so long ago it has become a dream.

Guarded

"Little birds   little urgencies   darkly clerical

     carry your notes to the child
practicing her quiet   in a forest

     far from the unfinished house
assigned her

fly through that bluish
     disassembling air

past bewildered ivy   chimes snagged
     in their hanging-strings

confusion of voices and peals   the sun wilting
     from its own heat

sing another
     arrangement"

Thinning

~

The girl was born with one
watchful eye
that could keep the village safe.
It was her sole purpose.
The eye witnessed a mother
sliding under
ice, her children
three small stumps
frozen on the river's edge,
the father slumped in shadows,
a rope around his neck.

What good was all that seeing
when she had no way
to tell it? Look at her eye now—
bitter, furious flower
infested by bees & flies.

Look at it
looking away.

~

For the fast I purchased three quarts
of juice. I'd be thin as a ruse.

                  A week of nothing

but Orange/Apple/Prune.

                   My system would be

clean. O gleaming discipline.

                  The scanter I became,

the greedier I got
for less.

~

Allotment: one square
of light & a half-crust & grapeskin
for vitamins

              Is that enough to leave a trail, to get back?
sufficient to keep me
walking to the room
where the scale waited

I could live on a bead—
shiny or dull—
and not collapse

Let the empty swings sway
Let streetlights dim

9

Let the wind and mousy-haired rain and even the sun eat away at me

~

That large rectangular restaurant window,
steam in the glass, wide tables,
grandmother & grandfather
from distant mesas and buttes sitting with me
eating as though we'd just seen a ballet.
       It was cold enough to be Christmas.
The spruce & scarlet globes hanging
& everything shimmering. My grandmother looking
directly at me. *She's thin*. My grandfather glancing up.
Strewn between us: handfuls of shatter & tinsel & tin
& meat & things I would never eat—

~

It was there they gutted earth
to lay two black tracks that couldn't touch.
There, the train. There, my seat by the window
where I sat on a real square of light—
tissue-sized. I felt my bones clear
as an X-ray, their starry knobs, the hard
weft and slope. With the first jolt
of the car, they thrummed.
       Half my weight dropped, loose
flesh lost, I was getting close to the marrow,

claiming my landscape—

the spectacular hill-bone of my wrist rising

as I turned in my ticket, my knee bulging

larger than my thigh.

                          The train lurched, its one yellow eye

fixed north where my mother waited

and would, for the first time, see me as I was.

~

Not eating was a sign

of grief

in our house: after he & he & he left,

my mother stunned

        thin as a rake, draped

in her wedding veil, bruised eye

        staring out,

her sisters dusting every corner,

refrigerator stark

& sponged.

        In my bed, I froze,

        coiled with snakes, wet with piss. Mouth

stuffed with a fist

        lest someone hear—

~

I was a gaunt circus horse practicing my getaway—

running for hours in circles

in the training gym

       around wires & nets & shovels for shit—.

                    Slashing at my forelegs,

one of those circus barb-hooks.

I rounded the next bend, windblown mane, ankles grinding

to gristlebone.

~

It's a quick trick:

Sink into the box—

       the mustachioed man

(jacket-tails flicked back, slick hair)

       saws through you slowly…

then it's rising time. Shake off the bone-flecks—you're

                halved, a lean miracle!

~

I slept in a house of hexagons,

the boxes we didn't unpack complicated

with twine & string & flaps—

It was a house of emergency exits,

no door. You had to be really thin

to make it out.

~

I fashioned a small snow-girl with one eye.
Caped in an icy sheen, snow-father leaned
off to the side, two brothers heaped like ghosts
unable to protect themselves from the sun,
snow-mother losing her figure
after the blizzard, trickling underground.

All winter their mouths filled
and dissolved. Sometimes as they melted,
they sunk under a headdress of starlings
and sparrows, twigs loosening from their sides,

eyes disappearing, small whitish-gray sockets
replacing them. I stared in vain
as though in my looking I could
save what was made to be
undone.

~

Once I so loved
the tiny pink-tulled ballerina
in the music box,

                           I cut her off at the feet.

       Poor stiff girl, perpetually
en pointe and lamed, toppling every time I tried

to twirl her

in my palm

while the stage whirled

without her...the tinkly music slowing to a drawl and slur....

~

I thought I could make it out by tunneling

through dirt, pushing

my star-snout through, leaving

a wake of spider-bits,

root-sprawl,

& the horrified faces of my family

standing at the mouth

of the hole.

They couldn't fit within

what I'd made, & I had no space

in there to turn back

to them.

I tunneled away

from houses, people,

flowers, birds...the hole

narrowing, my hands & body

falling into a rhythm

of my own

making.

~

I circled, circled the campus—*Where's
the carcass, the feast?*—greedy for the fat
double digits of the scale I stood upon....

I leaned hard into a book...words—my breath,
my light—blurring
in a dark wash of ink.

Farewell, *meadow* & *stoplight*—
Farewell, *starfruit*—
A collarbone in every poem I wrote.

Wedged between grocery shelves & bins
of loose bulk, I couldn't choose a morsel.

         At nineteen, reverent
& ashamed, I emptied a box of laxatives nightly—then drank
a syrup that would heave my guts up
through the throat.

        Who is that figure? What is
her name?

~

The people were so hungry they ate
dark plate after plate
of what I fed them—

without complaint—even
asking for more.... *Too heavy, too heavy* they hissed,
when I picked up a fork.

~

I lowered the blinds, sat
in the lack—

diminished, slack, grotesque—

just a body in the dark relieved
of its reaching, free

of its brain, its heart.

All mine I whispered
to the swelling empire
of emptiness—

~

The hand-that-was-mine
took a reflex-
hammer to the hard knot of knee—.
No kick.

Pliers quietly undid

the wires of Appetite.

A donkey's head in a cage
brayed & brayed. A test
of endurance not
to drop everything & save it.

The world was fixed as a crumb
on the tongue.

The stethoscope a pendulum
dangling—

steal a scalpel, pare more
flesh. Drape

another sweater over
your summer bones....

~

Is that a boy or a girl
      the child asked her mother while looking at me

I became absolutely perfectly silver in that
moment

I turned sideways I
vanished

~

What was I
that I chose not to float
that I lay thick with mollusks
my mouth filling
with algae I neither swallowed
nor spat

that I chose not to eat

like an animal
sickened on the salt of upheaval

I believed
each ounce I weighed
had an equivalent
grief

or was I human—
gagging what was
salvageable

I made a god—
annihilation—
I offered her bones
& she ate nothing
but fire fire
& whatever wind it was
that failed in that moment

to lift me
from the dark
strangle of weed

and push an oar
toward me

~

Remember the days of no
calendar no
future—relying on
the thin quavery finger

of the scale to settle
on a low stolid number

maybe 80
or 70—

concave enough to hold the real
jewel! To be glimmering pure and null....

In a blur of dream,
I imagined 60—the needle
trembling leftwardly, lower—a near invisible stinger
hovering
clean, sharp—decided
in its angle—one last

shudder to the left—

~

How did you make it back?

        asks the stone lion I pressed my body against
             before blacking out—

        asks the forking wisteria of my mother's forest
        where I retched repeatedly after eating—

      asks the sealed book I lay against

whose blood, scorching inside
with a life I shrank from, was my blood—

How did you make it back? echoes the last glass
      of milk I didn't drink.

~

At the hospital's check-in desk, they took my name. My mother
trembled, the nurse handing me
the yellow wrist ID for the children's ward.

you don't have to
do this you know my mother cried *you don't have to*
go inside we can

go home what do you want to do

Looking away from her, I turned
down the shining corridor on my pin-thin legs,
past the medics in green, the silver IV machines, tubes
& sacs swaying—

I carried my bag into the room.

~

Thank you for the cherries I wrote
my father, my throat still too thick
to swallow sweet bits, the girl
in the hospital bed beside me scowling
at my gift. The next day the whole basket
vanished. The girl brooded, skin
marked up where she had tried to cut
herself open. *They pulled me back*
for what? She looked my way. *Nobody*
gives a shit about me. Nobody
visited her side those months, while mine surged
with people & flowers & chocolate
I couldn't eat—*have it, have at it* I said
but she took only one, watching me warily,
calling me *Skinny* as I folded myself up on the sill looking out
at brick & alleyway, dumpster & anemic
yellow trees.
　　　On the day she tried to kill me,

21

her hands scarred rough & tight around
my neck, hissing threats, I hoarsely
issued reasons for her to stop. I spoke with the calm
of one who knows herself. *But you don't even want
to live* she cried, dropping her hands,
& I took my first full breath.

~

The women are trooping over hills, through
fields & rivers. They splinter as they stride, narrow
between trees & sparkling. Their eyes harder

than glass, than bone. Women trooping, brushing
against railings & mirrors, you would think their elbows
could cut through iron & glass, but iron & glass are

smarting their calves & thighs & necks & lips.
Even the rain is on parade—delicately tinkling
& cutting the women ever-so-lightly as they troop & thin

en masse over bits of glass & diamonds & caulk, bearing
gleaming compacts & glass jars of chalk. A glimmering
glass set—. How brightly the women thin in the gloss—

poised, swallowed by dumb reflective
surfaces with a sheen that stuns—.
(O Shining Epidemic!)

When the sun
drops low & the women lie safely
abed, their skin covered by glittering gauze,

their hard eyes focus solely
on themselves as things that need
thinning, weapons that will harm.

~

In deep green spring—
skeletal, draped
in thick shawls, full sleeves,

in my emaciation—
kneeling in sweet grass,

I was sealed, almost holy, cloistered
from men, from women.

     I had made myself
genderless.
     Lovers sailed past,
arm-in-arm, ample with flowers, I smelled the largeness
of their skin, felt their hands, their lips...
     a bird inside me
widened its beak—

Harlem-Hudson Line

In the yellowed glass, you can glance
at your face only when dark. And it looks back, more
sadly or severer than you thought. But beautiful as the dying
light. And more so in the rain when light is flat.

      You turn a frozen bend. In need
of alarm and flame—something to jolt you past the dragged
dark to the steamed-in car of memory. You sniff the track.
Oil and piss. Heat ground up by wheel. Some animal
lives there. Some animal that bared its teeth against bone
without swallowing.

Wolf & Root

I.

You can tell the wolf is sick——bluish

                steam rising from its flank——tail lain flat——
thronged by birds in medical masks.

                Its one yellow eye weeps hard salt.

You can tell it is sick, ridden

                with stench and itch, so in the pit it won't
twitch or flick off flies.

                At an operable distance, the birds perform their surgeries.

II.

                My father is impatient with the fork——
        roughs up its silver,
            skids it across the tablecloth
to where my mother's head is buried
under a napkin.

        I was conceived at this table.

III.

How might I manage—

      freeze mother and father on their stretchers so they will stay
                figures of the past—

how might I

        say *no harm done*
        let the wolf breathe

how might I not start

           at every word as all words

                    these days are suggestive

IV.

Star-pedigreed: its sharp nose, elegant
drop of fur, long curls down bony legs:
        the wolfhound was the dog my mother bred
inside the rattly kennels, inside our narrow house—.

Wolfhound in the hallway. My father finally home.
I'm trying to squeeze past the flanks of the dog

to get to him in his suit,
his dark distracted glasses,

but the dog presses me against the wall

29

and my voice doesn't manage

to rise high enough
before he disappears into a pleat of light.

       Someone said *she hounded him*. Someone said *he slunk off*
      down the oily streets with lipstick on his cuff and his lip.
Someone said
       when you were a child you never spoke.
       We all thought something was wrong with you.

V.

       Sniffing my skin picking me up from the train   she said
you smell like your father

       Picking me up from the train   he said
what has your mother fed you
why are your dresses stained

you sound like your father   she said
    dropping me off at the train   *you're slouching like him*

Dropping me off at the train   he said
           you could give me a call once in awhile
           don't drag your feet it's a beautiful day

don't tell him anything about me
           she cried driving me away

VI.

Come, hangdog shovel. Come, anything—
                    gate-hook, rake. Take
to that root wired deep in the earth, its dirty traversal,
                    its fang-drip, its stark length embarrassingly naked,
shredded
dirty webs of littler mistress-roots
                    clinging to it—
                                        the delicate threadworks fanning out
                                              pull easily,
but it won't budge. And when I hack at it
                    there is no blood.

VII.

I have strapped myself to a bed of dirt.
I have become a yard of cruel secrets.

                    What can I give you
mother, father
that won't wilt in your hands.

VIII.

I wanted to see the wolf, I had milkflower
for it—
                    but the fox arrived instead,

its mouth full of weeds and dead bird,

beautiful trotter, whisk-away tail, quick-fire-
brush, glimmer, fur piece on little feet
at dusk.

Dusk is a curtain my mother disapproved of.
She devoured my plate
before it was set.

At her behest,
I reached for an invisible glass.
I drank a bowl of soot.

IX.

Wolfmeat in the larder, a peppershaker of birds
      what to eat   what to eat

distended belly of the bell that has swallowed its tongue.

      What to choose from the shelf:
tentacles, barnacles, the seal's worried eye
        and then which spoon, what plate, napkin or not—

      how much to take....

The root again. Esophageal—as if in my throat—.

X.

    Tableau:

          a stricken Medea in the kitchen, my mother

                      raising her knife

toward my father's closed, smeared face.

    This will be a painting she hangs in her living room

    and points at incessantly.

        Down the tracks from her house,

    between visitations,

he sleeps all day in his bloated city,

getting up only to pull down

the blind.

XI.

        My father went waltzing off his birthday boat

        collapsed drunk in the dunes.

My mother went waltzing off a diving board

smack into the Arctic—everything so achingly cold and clear

        she could see right through the world

and I was part of it.

XII.

Above the field where the wolf lies,
a bell won't stop

       clanging. And the clouds around it

sink and rise.

       A clang and a clank. Dead
father and all your charming manners,

       I will give you a frame.

Father who says: *You will never have love*
until you work things out with me,
step inside—

       I will give you a small chipped cup to hold

       your sobs.

XIII.

Father, the father
you slung over your back
stunk of gin
and weighed what a shadow does,

       but you bruised
from the weight of him.

Mother, the mother
you kept in your head
like an axe in an icebox

covered her chairs with plastic,
closed her curtains tight.

There was nothing I could do right.
She had no music
in the house. She had a nothing-smell.

XIV.

In their dream coats
my grandfather and grandmother stand
on the floating pier

awaiting their daughters and sons
their eyes cold   hands flat against their sides

two oars
and a basket of dry fish at their feet

the boots they are wearing   heavy
with chains

the boat clanks and scrapes
the dock   its mouth full of rope

XV.

A fatherless house rises like a ship

in the forest.

You can fit a family of wolves in the hold.
Unvarnished cedar,

       unfinished wiring.

       The mother doesn't look up—
her hands grip a helm

       that won't cease spinning.

XVI.

Waiting for a yellow bus at the edge
of milkweed

in my slightly stained, slightly

       torn dress, swirls and zags of purples
and greens. I was trying to grow my hair long then—

                she zoomed down the drive in reverse

                spitting gravel,

                grinding a gear, late for work—

screeched to a stop before me,

       leaped from the car, yanked

       a comb through my hair

       there there

                I was barely present.

She jumped back in, roared

away,

                                     left a small hiss.

XVII.

Little white teeth
               that could exact
                       little white marks on my wrist.
In their corner of the porch, two raccoons are furious
and unafraid. I am between them
                     and the seed-bag. They snarl, lumber closer,
glotted with pus.

How fragile my screen, how little
it does to keep the masked animals away.

XVIII.

Gleaming dark as a bomb in the yard beyond,
               the machinery that makes the house tick
is exquisite. A kind of generator. My habit is to stiffly circle
its pretty tripwires. My habit: avoid talking about it.

               My new house is neither straw
                     nor brick. It grew around me while I slept.

A wolf lives in it—
                   his eyes are closed as he devours

flies, their peppery wings frenetic,
bits of shit falling from them.

My throat as I sleep fills with something
dry and incessant, grievously sworn, fattened
                    on injury. I dream of three horse-skulls
                              nailed over the front door, a pig-foot
as a knocker.
The wolf is my private
companion, I think—all mouth and yellow eyes
following me from bed to table to sink
                              to wall
                              to the faucet clamped so tight
I imagine nothing
ever flooding from it.

XIX.

The whole car stutters
and jerks when my father shifts gears— we're apt to go
all over the road, apt to hit
                              something. I say in a small voice   *dad.*
He is oblivious, switches
                    on the radio, turns to me
with a grin   *I'll have to teach you to drive*
not like a woman.

Thirty years later, I creep into a car hooded
by white tarp and dusk so I'm triply

38

covered, guzzling wine from the bottle.

      I am earnest as gas.

The sunshield's collapsed and I'm growing

with darkness, spreading with wine, growing and spreading, becoming

a vine, filling the car with night.

XX.

My mother taught me how to touch

her Borzoi—*gentle, gentle, go with the grain of the fur*—.

They were so thin our neighbors thought

she was starving them. I pressed my cheek close,

to hear their hearts—.

They were bred for chasing fox and wolf

my mother said. *Not for human love.*

The first time I saw her cry

      was when the dog slid under the ice

and didn't rise.

XXI.

The wolves circled the house

wherein my father and mother impossibly held hands.

My father clutched my arm until the final minute of the visit then jumped heroically from the train as it slid from the platform.

My mother bare-handedly grappled the snarled bittersweet that would eat up all
the light around my windows.

The fires they set! More for beauty
than for warmth...

embers everywhere....

XXII.

On our fractured raft
        mother hunched
        over one oar
father leaning
into the other

        my Unstoppables!
        I'm looking up at you
        from my huddle

—and you
        having forgotten the provisions

rowing nonetheless
moving us over
the inevitable water—

XXIII.

Spiky venomous split-haired root—
     stubborn thing, as stubborn as I.

     What might I pull from the dirt

that will not be harmful or harmed,
that will not recoil or turn toward me
                    a face of disapprobation,

     that will make my hands calm,
     that won't be a mistake.

XXIV.

This afternoon the sealed
           dry smell of the maternity ward
wafts over the garden
then swirls around me, my dedicated hands
       gloved for the removal
of the root.

     Strange, lovely petal, memory—
     hospital—

where I stayed
     alive with child
       with possibility.

I drifted

                              amply from floor to floor

in my green silk robe

            ready to deliver.

XXV.

One blow and the spade

            cleaves

            through the pith

of the root

                  soft with rot

                      red ants streaming out

crazed

        by the light.

They'd built their home there.

        What business of mine

                to shake loose those lives—

XXVI.

Hearts ticking fast, the children look
for bandages to help their hurts. They gather sticks

to keep the tomatoes upright. Holy basil, mottled
green and purple, fills their mouths.
The dirt's surprisingly

rich. There's a village of stones
caked dry by my feet. I disentangle the delicate
roots of new shoots. I flick off thrips
from bold, bright blooms.

An influx of worms. Deft spades.
Soft parades of moss.
One defiant slug.

XXVII.

My son sees it first, half-
buried in dirt: stick like a wolf—
agonized mouth, ravaged eye,
three legs. *Pick it up,* he says
get it away.

I lift it and carry it
to the porch,
dunk it into a waterbowl
till bits of bark and dirt rinse off.
What should we do next with this
poor old wolf.

If you tuck it under sweet needles

sing it a lullaby, then tiptoe off,
it will drift to sleep.

If you break it in two and toss it
into the woods, it will grow
ferocious and lonely.

If you cradle it in your arms
then return it to the tree it snapped from
it will circle aimlessly and die of heartbreak.

If you keep it covered with needles
it will sink and rot.

If you take it into your sleep,
it will grow another leg, another eye,
become strange
enough to fly.

Searchlight

On the platform she holds a dusty searchlight
grazing with yellow the corners, tiles, dirt
of this dim underground station. The subway's

      waterlogged, flooded with shadows. A tall thin figure poles
through the ripples to keep itself moving.... The searchlight's now widening,
its glow exposing

men tucked under the platform, men
ensconced in walls, all men shrouded
whether mummified or homeless,
towels wrapped round their waists, bare-chested
as Pharaohs, or stuffed in oversized coats, men
with roses dangling from their grimy mouths,

      but she can't find in the throngs a father. The men are clay-gray,
still as the dead. She drops the searchlight and climbs
a rope ladder above the glint of water, that awful blowfly-green.

      She hopes to reach the street.... Somewhere above he might be
passing storefronts amid a flurry of strangers,
but now the ladder's swinging wildly—is it her weight?—over whatever's
alive in that awful water....

      And the men, roused from their stupor, rise
and reach for its rungs and hooks. She fears they'll
drag it all down, her with it, or topple
into a frothy filth of dull-eyed carp—is that what's living?—or they might split
the pole of the tall thin figure—putting an end to the rippling....

But a second ladder falls from above,

the men scramble for it, dripping. As they pull themselves up, they merge

into one large man, his ladder swaying close to hers. *Is he her father?* Already

he's dissolving....

Trains are sliding underwater and through blurred window-squares,

many fathers tilt on the seats, draining bottles into their mouths,

their wet mouths....

A soft orange light rests on their bare ankles. It is

an interior light—

a wish. The color of the street. To get there she must drop

from the ladder, she must sink under—

Hymnal

Book in my hands——thin
& sleek.

      Something watchful
outside my window, poised
         to snatch it away.

Word floating up
from the white sea of the page——
       tiny horse,
        inky hook from its mouth and tail,

& the undersea blossoms trumpeting,
       their vines
              unfurling…

Whelk of syllable,
silk against my cheek, the book is
       ballast. *Grace & Bless*:

       something to do with someone
knowing me without me
       having to speak.

~

Once I loved
my father when he said god was
air & flowers

god
not heavy above me—

                    not for the taking...

~

God as ocean, god as net—god as negotiation
between them—

                    my family
foundered.
                    Tabernacle-gulls gone tuneless.

        My father & I not looking
at each other, stricken,
at our stations, fish teeming, streaking through us.

        What called us to float up,
disoriented bobbers? What pulled us back
to the wreck?

A seahorse for my father, gallant & awkward—

A ghost anemone for me, surviving by wavering—

~

I was taught to snub dad and god—
but did they force hot pokers
into women's mouths
to shut them up
      or blow through tenderly
in their blue monks' hoods
      & feathery shoes that skimmed over
fields, bullets falling
hard from their pockets
obliterating animals and flowers....

      At times, I waved to them:
did they intend the damage?

      I was a weed—
      sturdy, stiff, difficult to pick—

my body
thrilling to the inexhaustible
wind....

I bowed before its passing,

then rose, opened my blazing mouth

& ate of it—

~

God was
air & flowers

god
not heavy—

~

In every room my father entered I vanished
        we vanished in every room
the room enters itself with a dignified air
        I vanish when I enter dignity
dignity vanishes when it enters the room

In every shame there is a room
        nobody's standing though it's standing room only
I enter shame & the room vanishes
        my father vanishes

angel angel angel shoo

~

Once I loved
my father —

        not for the taking...

~

      When would he show?
Or would he. Hunched on a bench
      under narrow tubes of warming-light,

I read until the pages illuminated
      the whole station....

      In my drawstring sack I kept
a pebble the size of his eye, with a stick I could use
to row myself toward him.

      Father, I'm rowing through air
      in tightening circles....

Appear
without guilt or guardedness .

~

Forbidden
to ask questions
          of his own father, asleep on a bench
in a child-park, my father forbidden
to help him,

               but a heart could gallop
through widening streets and fields where clouds
& asters & fire hydrants & wheels & snails
meant—in the moment they were
noticed—

               something holy.

~

air & flowers

          not heavy above me—

~

God
& this circus. God glittering, faltering on the trapeze.

God in clownpaint.

No one looking at him, but god center ring, drifting down
in confetti.

Elephants wordlessly circling
at the hook's behest. God in that hook.

God and his tidy tricks. The red dogs rise in unison, raise their paws, bark.
God, the eye of the bullfrog in a box....

The elephant with the fierce squint—nipped by barhook—heaves his body
onto a drum, raises his trunk. God in that trunk.

Hundreds of doves rush out of a black hat, god rushes into it. Fumbling in
velvet curtain-folds, god breathing heavily from a mouth.
God rising in faint snores.

God messing with ropes. God hanging a human body from a wire. God in that
wire. God dazzling himself to oblivion.

No matter the sugarlump, no matter the lace, god refusing to look
up. No matter the acid-tipped rods at the tiger's throat. In the bluish-green
lights, god sawing himself in half. God as gold dust.

God rearing up in a white blast, a white scream. Rabbit-god,
tenderfoot god...

god in that elephant's enormous brain.
God in the father and daughter seated in this corner of the arena,
watchful, detached.

The elephant has been detusked. His face
pitted, caved in. One eye is rageful. One is weeping.

He is looking right through us.

~

The dream-father digs a trench,
        shovel heavy
with clumps of silt and grass and muddy water—when he stops,
        I slip near him,
stooping to peer at a small form
        barely visible in the mud-squall,
the size and shape of a squirrel hunched
        in prayer, but when we look harder, we see it is a cat—
deep green eyes, stiff body. We fear
        she is dead, but she leaps out of the water,
skittering off, agile, bright.

Now the father's face like the king's
        from the ancient story is wrenched—
half in tears, half in laughter.
        And I have no face. I am the dreamer.

Magnolia

A wedding broke out in the magnolia—
      fever of white gloves, distressed wind.

The bells hung upside down. They'd choked
      on their own tongues.
Hung too, on unspeaking terms

with the air, I acknowledged the impasse—
      I wore a dress of paralysis.

Then all her little white dresses lifted as one—
      as though on signal—a four-year-old

          girl tilting up her own dress
               in the living room, opening up
          like an umbrella to her mother's

          lover, her face, god I can't even
               imagine it, sweet and cold,
          methodical, desperate, trying

          to woo him—.

               Maybe I don't want

a voice at all. All this mouthing in the magnolia—
        thin cries—too delicate to tend. I think

of a sea and its glistening foams and cascades
        hundreds of miles off and its whales' limbic
thudding through water,

        their intelligent eyes bright with salt.

Rushed wind…
        white rushing petals…
                the ransacked air.

This Time Autumn

I.

Daughter-I did-not-have, come
to the colony collapse
        in our backyard—wasps
crawling in slow gold
demented arcs over the hive half-
glued to the branch,
        not eating any more, not building
their home.

        Move closer—the bewildered wasps don't break
from their parade....

        And there's the brother-you-did-not-have:

        bolting joyfully across
        the grass yelling about kites—.

Life there! Life! And craving...

our wasps keep looping, making
nothing of themselves.

II.

    …remember tumbling out
in ruddy clots & strings
& rubbery approximations….

                This time, last autumn.

A mouth a pinch of dust
could stuff.

III.

Daughter undone. Daughter who wasn't:

    I bank with other
    fish, flattening one cheek
    against the mud, turning the other
    to the glistening air.

              My one dark eye
    discolors, shrivels to a speck.

IV.

Open the cabinet door—no plates, no cups—
but on one shelf: little footsteps in the dust—
    a child has walked through hungry—
follow her—

is she in the storeroom beyond the blowing curtain

or in the unlit corner

where piles and piles

of petals

are stacked unevenly—

—turn with me quickly—

is that fish, bird, flower creaking around us?

—keep moving—it's possible she's just up

ahead.

V.

Inside her room the shadows are stuck.

She recites her nightmares

in the half-dark: *mother*

walking bewildered through the pieces, draped

in a bedsheet,

a mountain

porcupine spitting its tiny arrows black

as rice into my hands—

my grandmother holding an empty tray,

my grandfather slurping his soup.

She opens

the calendar, sees dust

in the boxes, x-marks through everything.

VI.

It was hard to be
tender, harder still
to find her mouth, to get her
to speak. As though she were a doll. Easier for me
to dissolve. Poof! Now we're just the circling
dust. Spinning off—what's

    to trust

    but Quiet: here it is in its best

    suit. Pacing,

    awaiting our arrival, its mouth

    full of flowers—

its wedding with Unsayable & Unsaid,
my constant suitors.

VII.

I am floating by, cloud for a face, pieces
                    of child folded into squares inside my body—

VIII.

my son says *I did not hit*

I did not bite I did not throw

the boy who did that is far away
in another land I'm a fireman

a working man an artist
it is the other you're after

that one doesn't speak your language
that one has a sister

IX.

At a particular time the baby ended. You ended.
There was no calendar for it, no mark.
Morning was dark in the hospital parking lot
when they took you—to where? I wish I'd asked. I wish
they'd given me a sack of you—a thumb-sack I could stroke
& carry in my watch-pocket.

When, in the moth-green gown, I looked
up from the strapdown, seconds after being sunk,
I asked: *Are you sure she's dead? If so, can you tell me*
why? The staff looked down. They had
no face for it, but the blunt doctor
paused at the door, before walking out.

X.

Once I went mean-mouthed,
spat out: I wouldn't have had
a *her*——. *Not*

> *in this ring, this pandemonium,*
> *these cutdowns, these pried-open-*
> *by-razors, the flatirons, the dumbing*
> *bells, the straight-bed circus, the parade of flat mirrors,*
> *not a her: fast-ditched, cinched*
> *wrung out, roped.*

I was afraid she'd be twinned. Afraid she'd be
mouthless. Afraid she'd not hunger. Afraid she'd
be halved. Afraid I'd tie myself around her, un-
willing to release either of us——

XI.

Little girl I could not love
because you ended
before you had a voice or ears to hear me,

I give you this armful of autumn, the flyaway
leaves, tumblerfuls of scarlet, the shimmering
tangerine bouquets in the branches & the cleaning wind

in lieu of the dark tight shoe of the mind, its

useless narrow

grief.

XII.

She chides me

for calling her little   calling her girl

I was not even a thumb-whorl   she cries

The leaves this time

last autumn

were bloody streaks of gold

She is the soft part of drapes I am looking through

she is the rain

that lashes away from this   lashes at that

XIII.

Sometimes she is patient—sometimes she hands me

a stack of the day's sufferings:

a vexation of arrows, a concave sky

& a tray of split violets & the mouth of a river & the blood's litany,

       or she offers me the mirror with its reminders:

my beautiful mercurial children, steady-eyed husband,

a few windows with light, sparrows....

She says she prefers not
to be my wagon
or my weight. She says kindly
I am not to talk to her again.

Worry

That bird I thought an insect was a bird—
its tiny body throbbed with sound, fast-heaving, clacking
music. Was it restless prisoner of air or pioneer?—
     manic in the branches, its nest a worry
of human hair, unstrung petals, who-knows-what, its throat insistent
with insects and forest and wind. Pulsing from branch to
branch with the recklessness that comes from dread,
it rattled between leaves till their spines shook.
     How do any of us survive the air, the manifold unseen—
floating discharge of the living, flecks, tittles, smithereens?
How do we shuttle through grievings that never had full lives, joys blanked out,
or the intermediary branches we didn't note, intricate and sturdy, abandoned
for a clearing: grass stunted in its tracks,
absence—and not collapse?
     When you appear, we watch the bird in the quivering heat by a house
where animals are glassed-in, furniture shrouded,
     the natural light pushed out.

We hold each other hard.

That such a tiny heart can carry all that noise
and fly.

Who to Me You Have Become

in memoriam

Lucy's in the garden. Milkweed-
      silk in her thin hands,
a book in her head....
      The wind lifts
her sparse hair—and in that tenderness she becomes
      something she can love: coppery-blue horse cantering
through weed-swung rain. Tomaž,
      not far away, passes his wrists through azure, through iron, through
the brain of wet blooms, a mouse in his sock. He's trampling
      the roots that are his veins, our veins,
electric, animal, loosely contained.
      Above these plots, the Moon is oracular and chalk.
Look away before she falls apart.
      We're in the garden too. Quiet as the bench on which we sit.
Not ghosts, though ghost's our parlance
      beneath this trellis of thin minutes.
Gray husks of gloves on our laps, dry
      mollusks. Climbing blue
wisteria frames us where we sit
      already gone before I can say who to me you have become, how I—
—have come closer. In your listening, I nearly
      hear my voice. And Tom is here now, Tom now there too—
in the garden in the rain, rain turning to early snow,
      by the Holy Basil, entwined in tomato vines,

cupping a snail in his gruff hands, placing it in the earth

      where it feels home. Tom

while the heart's being torn. Tom—

      into little coppery-blue pieces—tiny heart-pieces—drifting skyward

as though—after all—love was just

      a cloud.

Reader

The young man read to me while the candle burned and I slept.

He was like a mother to me, reading through the night, the roughed-

up clouds breaking outside our dark window, sirens gathering

red blurs in the dangerous section. He read the wrenched faces of flowers,

the cursed birds. He read me into dream. *A yellow door, a glass person.*

He read, the rain splintering as it fell. So much of his life cleaving.

He read the candle burning beside him but he was also

reading to the candle reading to the night reading to me as I slept,

secretly a candle. The candle had a heat that hurried down pulling

everything down with it, pulling its own light down with it—it had pulled me

to sleep and dream as his reading did. So much of his life cleaving. The words

he read had returned from war, trembling, rich with blood, staggering

from page to page, each a historical moment. The young man read me

into a dream. *Horse in a glowing red field.*

                            Like a mother, he'd half-covered me

with his coat near the lamp with the broken shade. So much of my life fractured.

In the closet beyond his voice, a row of glass jars, something in them slowly

turning gold. He read to me as though I were six years old, his coat pulled

up to my chin, my hair smelling of roses and hay. No wind in the trees outside

the house. Night hurrying underground as though with flame, as though with

thought. No word that is not wind that doesn't carry its effect. The words, too,

are going under. So much of my life cleaving.

You read me into dream as though I were six, your hand rested on my head, my hair smelling of hay and roses, rain splintering as it fell outside our dark window. Something like candlelight inside our skin.

"You're brave to take on exiles" Beckett said

In the icestorm   ice dropping out

of the sky   *Meteorite Ice* our mothers said

On Wish Ave.   I am heading toward you driving

toward you   blue tailpipe smoke in tow

Now the ice is   little fish-bones

tinkling down   on my windshield

an occasional shank   of ice clanking

but mostly on Wish Ave.   the sounds are small

and light a little frightened   as though deigned

impermissible   even in slightest action

such as dropping themselves   through tender air sharp trees

deigned impermissible   by our Icy Mothers our little bones

tinkling down   Violent is the wind that won't

budge Violent   the blocked-up stoppered Wind-

of-our-Mothers   Heading to you in the ice

storm I can't find   my blood frozen

incapacitated by ice   but I am moving
in a clear direction   that I know by heart

determined unflagging   as is my sense of failure
that is in part moving   me toward you

"Thank you for sending me Silence"
said Beckett   I can see you through bare trees

Dear Reader

Dear dear dear dear dear dear dear dear dear dear dear dear dead
                    diamond orifice in the night .   sharp heated mouth
moon-white   Dear star above

              dark vulvic nightflowers   drenched   petals
wrung-out in flight   difficult as letters are   folded in the fields
              of the heart

When we wake   we wake   my hands on your chest   your
              hands over mine   dear in all this   gesture and sign

Now we're heading toward a yellow door through several rooms to a window
then the fields   There is a   threshold between   longing   and need

appetite and hunger   horses behind or before a fence
          dark liquid eyes   serious faces   flanks pricked

by flies   The horses in a fine summer rain   feed   pulling at wet tufts
There is music in the field .   cymbals strings

Next to you I feed the horses .   Inside me lives a winter light
          from decades of nights   spent walking inside and out dear dear dear

dear   doors   passageways   fear   I am not asking you to follow the
memory-me nor am I able to go   to the rooms where you live but tonight

we're moving   light and rich as amber   in a world that
has disqualified us   for loving as we do   We're moving with

a slow light   as pipefish
and seahorses   clouds now racing slightly blue   thickening   The wind the

wind too   you send me   Wrung-out in the field   I am
tired-eyed   now and unto   unto

the end   the end of this skin   folding creasing again
          the damage   evident

Dear dear dear   we are kneeling now   in the shaken light
          in a room   where the bed   has an exact corner

Go to the window that holds   the moon's face   Read to the glass
Dear dear dear   the moon   is cutting tonight

beneath its soft-lit swoon   Put a padlock on it
                    No no it is not running away   but it is

shy as a horse   slow   and kind   in its reluctance
leading us through another memory   in our disqualified light

to the world that has failed us

Ruby

You pour a ruby liquid

       from the glass flask that was your father's

into the mouth of the shadow who has fallen

       from her horse   She's fallen flat and

spreading   She could occlude the sun

       Don't let your mind go

there   the people whisper

       as they die in the tunnels of their bodies

Tunnels lead to light   the people say

       while their bodies crack like plaster   fall

apart   It wasn't dust they were made from   it was live flies

       with hoody eyes

You keep pouring the ruby liquid into the shadow

       though it isn't night and shadows have an unspeakable

sadness precluding drink and food   The people envy her for being

       near invisible   The ruby liquid will cloud

her throat   faintly redden her   How lonely you are

       for someone   What are the people now saying

Guide her hand around the glass to make

       a picture from the condensation

Streak her hand through it   The shadow

is a child of bleakness   Streak her
shadow-hand through what becomes
of water   Later you'll visit the river

Going

Going now to dark, going now to write in the dark
love-cabinet. The red fish like a stuffed glove on the desk,
going out of gray all the time, gray seeping back. I like Beckett
when he scoffs white and black. Going in out of light in out
of my undercover love. Now seal the window. Our smells already flown—

    soft flowers of air or ash-tufts undone. The sound inside
the walls a heart. There's the night in your voice again, snakewood
alive in the hearth. Nobody spoke when the smoke rose. I'm going now
to dark. Going to lift the coverlet and feel your face there even when it's
not, going with my solo hand inside to still a willow
by its thirsting root. There's another page of light—all trees are stately—

    I don't care how slovenly some think they seem, snagged by fishline,
straggling roots half-drowned, bruised knuckles with a tight blue sheen—
all trees are venerable citizens and are divine. I head into their dark
love-cabinet with you, a morning of roughshod stone in out of
the dark love past the last bright bursts of thready lavender-blue
asters before we disappear again.

    Going now to write in the dark. I feared your heart
was footfall down the hall, someone or something trying to undo
us. Watch us watching the autumn trees in the wind laughing and losing
pieces of themselves. We are alert and high and bright, carrying the air
well, carrying the air not on a stretcher
but in our hair, its high bright pieces in our hair. Beckett

    was correct—he was inching back into gray when it fled. Where the dark is now, we lay on a slab of wood in the sun. Where the dark was then,

now a lit glade, love-cabinet

    we are tendrils of light in the dark of it.

Scorch

This—another   slow train winding darkly
    in first morning hour   This—scotch
This—blurred burn   The children sleeping
    and the moon   the longer in its harbor
no longer so irregular

    and I in my harbor   of loss and desire
    am rocking tied to the pier   the porch has become
With such rushing wind   we must be by the sea
    I am rocking without my body like water as you are

rocking without yours   This moon behind the porchscreen
  made of particles   the screen   the wires hitched in it   tiny particles
your face   and mine   particles gathering
    as we speak   shiny tidbits   of words

       Your voice corresponds with the night
    This is why I listen well to you   Upstairs
the children have pulled blankets over their heads   they are two low-lying
  hills so small we can hear them breathe   from below   It is October
    the purpose in the shape itself   and not in reason

Who could explain   Could any
    explain the gold of scotch   your wrists glowing

on the porch table   phosphorescent   *loss and desire*

Sometimes you become a shadow   I am wishful for
      or a ribbon of light   the moon is helping to make
I can't feign any understanding   but recognition
      Your voice in the night   The next distant train

clattering over tracks three neighborhoods away
    breathes heavily   How is it we are this close
to the moon and the night and the children
    I can't see that train now gone to silence foregone its nervous
twisting smoke

All our disasters—   The heart of the world—
    You are my favorite flower of the dark
I am afraid of the trains and hours that might take you   the scotch that might
    petrify your throat anything that might flatten you I am afraid for
your heart and your voice rich with night   I am trying to listen well
enough to keep you here   at harbor   You are another ocean bordering
    so many islands   *desire and loss*

I am not qualified to talk of light this way
I have not the quantity of whispers

sufficient to meet the sea   Its tiniest whitecaps like meadow asters
    at gunpoint buckling under   We are a fable
on the sunporch drinking scotch   the moon more regular
    in its irregularity   *loss loss*

There are scant retrievals crumbs of light   the particles that give us shape whether or not we can feel   iota   jot   tidbit

Here's another—

                   and another—

Funeral: For Us His Gold

after Gerald Stern

.

The insect was yellow with crumpled black-banded legs

    and shellacked back that would outlast us

    and wistful eyes from what I could discern on that trail between fields,

and we laid him out in the open air under a sky fast-blue with change, wedging

    a leaf beneath his triple-belted belly so he didn't rest on plain dirt,

    and we placed two cloverblooms by his head and he was old

you said, could tell by how definite the stripes were, how complete

    the patterns bold and dark, almost engraved,

and he was beautiful in that pasture of thirty-three cows and we drank

    milk in the blaring heat and ate the cake you'd made. We were

    the only humans there—unholy-seeming things with two legs, dismal histories—

drinking and eating around his elegant husk,

    and from the furze, fellow insects rose, a frenzied static around our bodies,

while he remained in situ an unremitting yellow, the color more

    vivid, louder now that he was a remnant. Was color the purpose here?

Yellow had alerted us to him, and we took care

    with leaf and clover to make his bed.

The insect's gold our togetherness, its death from which we fed.

First Smile

for Oliver

More beautiful because without intent
and seldom. Little spits of rain we are—
little dazzlers. Ghostherds from cottonwood
speed through the air, a gazillion seeds
in the fluff, the teeming soft of it, mobs
of birds pulsing skyward through their fog,
monogamous to death—as beautiful as this:

your small smile without intent. As everything first
seen and recognized is most beautiful—
sudden hummingbird, without agenda
or wariness. What we bear—the dust,
the dead blown by the dead—briefly lifts
before that bright infinity.

Small House with a Blue Door

for Milo & Oliver

i.

Under a blue errancy, I haul
seed to the feeder. I haul
sun and rain

through this field into the next.
Nothing around me shall famish.

The ditch cradles a fat fox.

In the lower stream, a fish skates through skeletal light—

Does your hair have bones a child asks.

ii.

        Later I find the thumb-sized possum
babies or fetuses—don't know don't want

                        to know—

nearly translucent.

        They'd been strewn—roadside—

                from the cleaved-open-body of their mother,

their miniature hands
frozen, mid-clap—.

The mother sank elsewhere, glittery with flies, fur heavy with summer.

iii.

The youngest dreams his fingernails are falling out—
thin petals
browning as they slip.

I don't want the fox to eat them he cries...

He doesn't want to see the stars or moons
or black clouds skimming the yard.

His mouth is a bud
when it's closed. When it opens,
I am devoured.

iv.

At the threshold: a mouse-skull
clings by a tendon to the wet velvet sack
of its body,

the size of a child's hand,
the one I try not to grip
too fiercely.

He says: I *am tired, too tired for food.*
(You think: *I am too tired to be good.*)

v.

Children are piling blankets over me.
One strokes my hair, one curls in my arms, presses
his face into mine.

vi.

Walkathon!
the eldest exclaims, face gleaming with recognition,
pointing at the front page,

a newsprint smear on his hand
like a smoky bloom, his eyes widening
at the miracle: other children

in the news, right before us,

walking as he did that morning—
the photograph of those children

walking in lopsided file, steered from school,
eyes tight-closed in the bright air, hands

resting obediently on their classmates'
shoulders, led away
through what was left
of noon.

The whole sky
void of its former color. Flags

lowered, limp on their poles like the bibs
we throw away.

Once, the child-slayer
lived on top of the hill, shrouded by woods.

vii.

The world announces coldly: *There can be no more figures.*
Here you are no longer a child.

viii.

Snow—

    . that white ongoingness

        obliterates

            the calendar's boxed days.

Two sons, two circus-walkers,
       gravity in their pockets.

ix.

             Give me a generous murmuring field—

not the demolished face of the possum
I've pushed with a stick
into the cottonwoods.

      My lullaby's on trial for being soft,
         my eyes for being hard.

x.

You walk through the children
and find yourself taller, heavier—

xi.

I check the underbelly of the porch for rats
for littered scraps I check the feeder

      I check the creek for rising   The sky for hawks

I check the crushed thing on the sunporch
who sobs in my son's dream   And the fly
            whose oversized buzz
keeps him from eating   I check

the starfish-stickered car seat for faulty belts   I check
the moon's thready eye that has witnessed too much
to regard my children

Fat robins flooding the field   *Check*
Milk   *Check*
Switchgrass by the electric fence

I check my face   the crib   the smell of the sheets

                        children

I check   their breathing   I watch for movement

xii.

The eldest carries a snag-
toothed saw, hammer, and wrench in a glowing vest
meant to keep him visible in night's
raw-socket black.

He assures me
the tools I love are not deadly.

Do you have a flower I can fix? he asks.
I can take care of anything that jams
or cries. The swing set. This plug. That torn
screen. Your flattened mask. I have a tool
for that.

xiii.

Two children stepping toward the perimeter—
    will they find you or a shadow there?

The sculpture called

Angel of Death lived in your house: wings tucked,
wooden shoulders hunched. His stooped frame, shadowy face
seemed human, seemed to need consolation.
You tried to stroke his cheek—
he was too tall and gaunt for you to reach....

Roy

"...your daughter is thinking of death, of

        suicide"

                Roy says   gin racing down his throat

She tuts   annoyed

        back turned

           from his "monstrous" words

Even when he curses   his voice is thin   wiring out

    from a squeezed-in place:

              small starved watchful voice

architect of my mother's house   (Where was my father?)

* * *

Downstairs I rise in a pale yellow bed alone—

        On no uncertain terms am I not   alone—

           Negatives of Forever   fluttering filmy

ghostly cards in my

hands   I don't know how to shuffle   My alone-ness not sacred enough

to carve into a tree

      but I spray-paint it on the stone walls in Ravenna,

Italy: *Sono Sola*

From the tomb-y distance   Dante looks darkly on:

      I'm circling memory   Roy's gin gently

leaking from his   dead mouth

      I siphon into mine

      (I managed to stay alive by not

          needing anything   )

* * *

Roy knew a little of me a little— at six I was an itty ghost then an awkward
swan wearing his whitish-blue button-down shirts as nightgowns—sleeves cut
off jagged as wings—oft-startled—Maybe he knew enough for me to know at
times I did exist—

      no recourse but to float—above Roy and his gin and glasses filled with
ice shuddering as though paper—and the birds Roy made from metal staples

Suicide
he whispered to my sleeping mother

      It was a dream of Paradise

Dante uneasy as befits a bust in a catacomb

* * *

But I as a child must have been something to fear.

I was small, jolted. So quiet you could hear the rattling.

I gathered cranesbill and hawkweed and flowers signifying death.
I gathered the live tree next to the scorched one.

Don't ask me to be reasonable. I gathered what felt right.

And I never sat anywhere lest I leave a dent.

The snails I made of mud and clay
unraveled, their eyes ungrateful.

Living in a slate basement, I had nothing else to make.

At least the centipedes were alive and frantic, if noiseless.

That gift from my mother,
a life-sized doll of me, I hanged,

I willed myself to watch slowly spin.
I didn't want pity to make me visible.
I wanted understanding.

Hail! Here's lank-haired-sealed-mouth me, on a stretcher stretching

away, cold as a poison berry

hanging from its branchy chandelier, transmitting

shadows without light

going every whichway,

belonging nowhere right.

My airiness

was the thing to fear. It could make a house collapse.

Move move they cried as I sat in the dust-

shaft, obedient to paralysis, a terror

for all of us, that nothing

could shake.   One wind-gust and the house

     broke into pieces around me.

* * *

Flushed brain of tulip   the garden

       seen through his drinking glass

       that changed like magic

       from gin to scotch

and both were gentle flames he drank there

among the weeds and foxglove and snowdrops

      where anger dampened
lovelessness dimmed
      where his voice curled a warm blur

and suicides became the tiny shields of leaves
upon the ground—shields

      of fractured bronze and twiggy bones,
      shreddy silver   love in the tarnish

Roy floating through purple crocus   Roy hovering over the brick

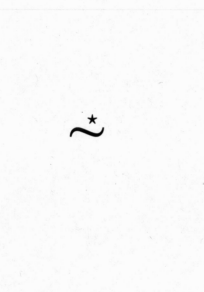

Meditation on Rain

In a blue collusion of dusk
and rain the sky's darkly shaking
like horsetails flicking

       off bloodflies. As you'd try
switching off half-truths that fed
on your skin, their little bites
       distracting you
from harder pain.

       Nothing a hoof could gallop from. Nothing to ride here
but air
       coolly passing from stable to woods—
each leaf a perforated heart—

to the front porch of the blue house. As you ascend,
       the steps darken behind you, night
has its own quiet stepping—it is not
       an abyss, not amorphous
as once you felt—.

How wavery the rain at the threshold—

Bird by the Blue Door

I.

Only the child's shovel will do—
        neon-green, simple
maple handle.

Behind barberry and cottonwood, I am private, tucking
the bird into snow, far

                from the house

that killed it when it veered out of its orbit.

Later I'll clean the shovel with yellow
fluid, smelling bright as nails.

II.

After the bird dropped with a thud,

        I wanted to work my fingers through the freezing feathers,
coax the wings to fan out,
        its thumb-sized heart too rapidly beating,

bleary eye half-open,

but there was no touching it.

At night, my child presses his cheek hard against mine,
his ribs against mine
        till we're doubly pulsing.

The wind's a small unbidden sound,
        not grieving.

III.

I could have waited for the fox to lick
        the bird's eye closed, nudge its weight from
my doorstep, then streak off,
        carrying the bird in its mouth
over the fields
        to where it belonged.

I could have studied the crenulations
        of the bird's underwing or sketched
with a charcoal stick its fine head. Or burned
        the bird to a teaspoon of ash and scattered it
over the lake.

IV.

Once I could hold someone
else's love so patiently,
distantly, you could hardly
        tell it was me loving.

V.

I have cried I have not cried enough

I have ignored the compass

        fractured the map with blindness

while the worms
        died in the earth they kept making

I have cried I have not cried enough

I blanketed my child
        before he could think to cover himself

I thinned myself as though I were a project

I blot out grief as snow does light

        I pass through mirrors—

VI.

the last day of february and the barberry and snowbirds
and surveyors' little orange and yellow flags flittering

my armor shiny bits of my helmet in pieces we are in pieces one

feathery piece of us dropped and I have been talking
so much god has vanished   my words   a little something   to bring
to a party

VII.

Beautiful fractal—
          bird with a blur for an eye, what did you
see before plummeting?—shadow wavering

at the threshold, glommed
          by light.

          Later—the shock
of snow you slid into
from my green shovel—the chilly
distances
          between branches where you might have perched
and twitched. Under mulberry trees sacked in white ash,

how handsome in your death-suit,
sealed clean—

VIII.

In spring, it rains and rains
and the water rises
from the drainage ditch, carrying
pitch and froth and mud and melting

      snow and sodden feather-sack,
the water spilling over
the bank, over the creeping things, the ivy,

         snagging what it hauls itself over, dragging
      the bulk toward my house...pulling everything
unburied

      closer to me, circling my ankles, insistently lapping....

Abandoned

What we built because we landed
where we did was shivering tent-like——.
      The crows flapping over-
head, our fathers and mothers
in their beaks.
      The fevered thread we used to stitch it
was inherited. Why had we stretched it
as we did? The many desultory pegs.

                      Didn't we hear

      the wind in its harrowed state distractedly
unpiecing it?
      To fog we went, to the bed
of estrangement, nest of stakes and knotted strings,
              uncertain and geometric.
                    How could we know our harm,
the violent shudder rippling through the mesh
as though it had nothing to do with us. It had nothing
to do with us.

We had abandoned it.

Couplets

Whose Voice is this   wrecked in the Sand?
A mother's   a girl's   a man's?

Salt spray its spirit broken up in waves
Whose voice   determined not to hurt a thing

too dogged to belong   in a body   Voice
awakening rattling   nervous as a husk

while the Sea reaches   through
its gagging froth   for the Voice

mouthless in static speaking
of how connection   fails us   how ardent we are

for repair   Some of our faces veiled
to ward off   bitter rivets of scorch and salt

Veiled mothers sons daughters fathers   Veiled husbands wives and the
child   too   already pulling a veil over his face

Where are his eyes?   Where where....
The Voices churn up   thrashing in a sea

118

then shudder to a halt——   thronged by an armory of

eyeless fish

      Walk quickly over the Sand to find   the image we've wed   we've

wived or husbanded   shimmering softly   there like a plea

leading us back   to the fractured waves

Is there a Voice   or Mind that can help

unveil the ones   I love   unveil the wounds

that have become   non sequiturs or   not-to-be-spoken-of

Veiled husbands propped on a barge
        Dry heart of the wind thrust open—.

Is it the Veil that corrupts their sense of orientation?
Their hands raw to the knuckle from scrubbing pans as if on Duty,

faces long and smooth and oval,
princesses' awaiting a kiss

The stars make a scrap metal city above
They must deaden themselves to get to the dead

Whose husband is this one? Husband of Absence? Blood trickles
from the barge   Good thing there's plenty of water to swallow it

From how they speak, you might think they don't want to be erased
but they seem to long for erasure, perfect space where nothing happens, and
nothing does

You'd think they were ink not chalk
You're afraid to touch them, afraid they'll shudder

        Dry heart of the wind split open—

Here is a sonnet I say *take it to your dead*

Rows of Veiled Husbands fork some chicken toward their mouths

stains spreading over their laps their skin   Their dead
eyes don't acknowledge me   *I must be dead myself*

I am bypassing the yellow line   *When I turn around*
you'll be a bouquet of roses

but my words weaken as I speak and their dead eyes don't look up
to meet mine

I can't manage the stain I cry   *I am always spilling on the dead's*
white carpets

Forget about that they say through the mesh
We have our boxed days and sponge as ammunition   They'll keep us safe from the living

With a pellet of bleach we'll kill snakes and all the garden   We'll scrub your smell
from the sheets so you'll forget to want forget to need

The veil around their mouths is turning yellow
Parts of the veil stick clammily to their cheeks

I take off my own veil and offer
it to them

I take out my throat
but the grief remains

121

The wife circles the standing dead men   lined up at the kitchen counter
waiting to feed   by the small screened window

milky sycamore outside   She feels guilty
when she looks past the men   afraid they'll vanish beyond death

She circles the standing dead   They're bandaged
in perfect X-mas ribbons in curlicues   their favorite day

They're waiting to be found   They want her around so she's circling
Here's one   wearing yellow latex dish gloves   He's forgotten to eat

O those who can't pick or carry flowers   those without
a thorn *What did you say what did you say I can't hear you what*

do you say? Now their mouths are moving really fast *What do you want
me to do? Just tell me* they say in unison *Tell me tell me*

~

A black moth   sooty wings   tragic beauty
twitching in one husband's mouth   O what agony he speaks fast then faster

I want more of the same of you more you the same the same you as then as now
The heart is everywhere and nowhere a furious madness disturbed

As he speaks his mouth keeps sucking up part of the veil
        stiff mesh-material   blowing it back out wet and hapless and pink

An addendum to the dead
                    What heaviness the house bore as it fled

"husband why don't you weep don't you weep husband
        why don't you sob

won't you come near to the star   the star in the jar
        husband the star of fate   or of disregard

behind the bed rattling and glowing a little
        not still   not dull   but a bit witless husband

hear the bell in the tower by the blue cloud   outside
        the shroud the snow makes for the crying tower   the birds

torn as gauze scrapped   by a breeze
        our children rustling in their sleep

cement-apt-to-crack husband   come soften with me
        the mattress is supple where you lie

bandaged in sheets   beside you I am always flowering
        tears   husband

can't breathe through these blooms   the house is another gag
        our children   restless

        with sadness   keyless quartet
of us   merciless love"

———

Maybe we were children when we first stepped outside
our own bodies first felt them as burdens, lopsided

from shouldering the broken wheel on the harder
side the father side the father's father's side the mother's.

Don't tell me anything, night-flower
in your fervent blooming.

Be wary of me now, night-flower, bow down.
The burnt forests beyond——.

Our mouths all scrolls
and secretive.

There were three stout bright buckles in the sky.
Orion's belt I said. *Just try*.

* * *

[Imagine him as your son who imagines the moon
falling down to the earth

landing inches away from his face
Inches he says

That moon absolutely gray
enormous

and cold
inches away

How little a child's face
without light

Absorb that
blue frenetic shock

Face the child now
our son]

The husband searching for the wife,
His voice corkscrew-tight.

A glacial deposit right outside
The kitchen window. Cold sum of it.

She said. He did. She bade. He hid.
He said. She did. He bade. She hid.

She gone to the sad gone to the heavy,
Gone to the flower in its drowned-out bed.

He gone, the sad, the harried, the flower
Drowning. Done for the god, done with

Suggestions, done stop gone yield.
Surely they move away from the self

As shadows shadowing each other's
Shadows, without an outward form,

Without the sound of hooves,
For instance, the sound

Of an approaching figure
Shortening the distance.

* * *

Other people appear! In the front yard one young man leaning forward mows
fast, gold hair blown back, mowing over the square plot where she'd planted
　　crocuses

They'll grow back she says to her husband also watching him and the other
workers milling *Will you no longer be mowing yourself, have you hired them? Yes*

but she a little shaken by the speed and the bulbs cries to the workers *Follow me*
so they do and they walk toward the backyard past yellow trumpet flowers hanging
　　low

their soft folds grazing our heads they are so musical they are also bells *How*
　　beautiful
the workers breathe as they pass into the backyard where she wants to show what

to protect but the husband has cemented a stationary bicycle and metal box onto
　　the grass
so close to her garden she thinks it's destroyed but no there is frittered dianthus and

red-eyed coreopsis spiraling yolky marigolds phlox and glad-handed milkweed
still alive! And while she may lament the gray inertia around them, the workers
　　listen

when she says *Please take care, there are blossoms* and the workers are those
the husband hired to labor for him the husband no longer this dream

Only flowers there to kiss—

~

Even the birds, anxious and tiny as hearts lifting up fluttering back—
even the birds—are veils—.

-------------------------I've moved closer to the narrow strip of light I've

    blamed the thing I hurt

Bared my light while scrunched eyes shut knowing nothing

but dark---------------------------

My brutal hiss of blue

------redacted humanhood

I've circled the orange scalp of the sun

---bade good-bye repeatedly the Sea

become a beach-slat beach slut

--------------knot of twisted eye

---------------knife-flash I am sliding out

of the drawer repeatedly

---or am I a troubled ocean wave

hurtling that shiny stuff onto the sand

~

The wound is bare today—its history exposed—
      flooded with centuries of sky—

ash-blue birds and plummeting specks,
      soft booming cloud, children—parents—

I sit on a bench—nothing
      to ask of the wound—naught required—

Wound-in-the-Open—
      somehow spoken for—

Jetting through Inconclusive, jetting past
sea-rocks, past the bleak-eyed to

a sky undisguised and cold—
whose sky? Jetting on these skis too fast to apprehend

a color. What shape is marriage
in, other than lonely as a buoy

that from a distance is bomb or hank of wedding weed or some
unnamable floating

longing for
definition now that the veil of fog has lifted

from the bright blank face of sky—
idiocy? Possibility?

This colorless dress too stiff to move freely in
too shroud-like to belong anywhere but in one place....

I will define you as Inconclusive—that it is
the relationship with the thing and not

the thing itself—where the veil lifts
the veil drops, fog is the breath

of the sea, the rising spray now

arcing now spewing. Wind is the body between us.

I am leaving an impression on the water that the water's

swallowing—

Coda: *Late March beneath the earth*

fanged root begins to snake—
in three sharp thrusts
I rout out a stub

toss it on a dry heap of yellow sticks
somewhat weakened

Once ravenous
in the bed

my arms crept up hung from the iron
frame   *Pull me out*
I cried

to no one   my husband gone where he was
my family melting away
and I

attached as a root to blight
or to what is
invasive O honeysuckle

O pretty and sweet
The hollow stems crowding out
light O soundless plague of the forest

Imagine somebody whispers
stopping that cycle imagine you
being the one

I lay abed my spikes softening unwitnessed
mouth adrift missing
a petal

Heave out each inch of bindweed
and what is left   A hole
too vast to be a hole

god-gutted space within the earth
nothing to push against impossible
to envision   There what could be living

I go into the kitchen for water   I await my friend
who has for years worked
his family garden

He who is kind
regards the root and starts
to dig—

Acknowledgments

Grateful acknowledgment is made to the editors of journals in which some of these poems appeared, sometimes in earlier versions or with different titles:

32 Poems, "Guarded," "Magnolia"

The Antioch Review, "Epidemic," (a section from "Thinning")

Colorado Review, "Supplication," and the section of "Couplets" that begins
    "'husband, why don't you weep…'"

Connotation Press: A Poetry Congeries: "Who to Me You Have Become," "Small
    House with a Blue Door"

Crazyhorse, "First Smile"

Indiana Humanities, "Hymnal"

JuxtaProse, "'You're brave to take on exiles,' Beckett said"

Kenyon Review, "Meditation on Rain"

The Laurel Review, "Bird by the Blue Door"

Michigan Quarterly Review, "This Time Autumn"

New England Review, "Going"

Pleiades, "Wolf & Root"

Poem-a-Day, "Funeral: For Us His Gold"

Thank you dear readers, brilliant poets, kind friends—Catherine Barnett, Chris Forhan, Dana Roeser, Natalie Solmer.

Much appreciation for your good care of books, beloved editor Carey (who speaks in poetry about poetry)— & much praise for the warmhearted, sharp-eyed AJB crew: the indefatigable Alyssa, Julia, Emily, et al. The gardens you plant!

For your wise guidance & unwavering listening, deep gratitude to Earl—

Grazie, Mamma, for a lifetime of supporting my words, for being my reader & editor, & for providing the resources that continue to help me get to the source—however (sometimes) painful for us both.

Love from the difficult depths to my families—

and to all—love—.

RECENT TITLES FROM ALICE JAMES BOOKS

Alice James Books is committed to publishing books that matter. The press was founded in 1973 in Boston, Massachusetts as a cooperative, wherein authors performed the day-to-day undertakings of the press. This element remains present today, as authors who publish with the press are invited to collaborate closely in the publication process of their work. AJB remains committed to its founders' original feminist mission, while expanding upon the scope to include all voices and poets who might otherwise go unheard. In keeping with its efforts to build equity and increase inclusivity in publishing and the literary arts, AJB seeks out poets whose writing possesses the range, depth, and ability to cultivate empathy in our world and to dynamically push against silence. The press was named for Alice James, sister to William and Henry, whose extraordinary gift for writing went unrecognized during her lifetime.

Designed by

PAMELA A. CONSOLAZIO

Spark
design

PRINTED BY MCNAUGHTON & GUNN